OUTDOOR
REPAIRS

OUTDOOR
REPAIRS

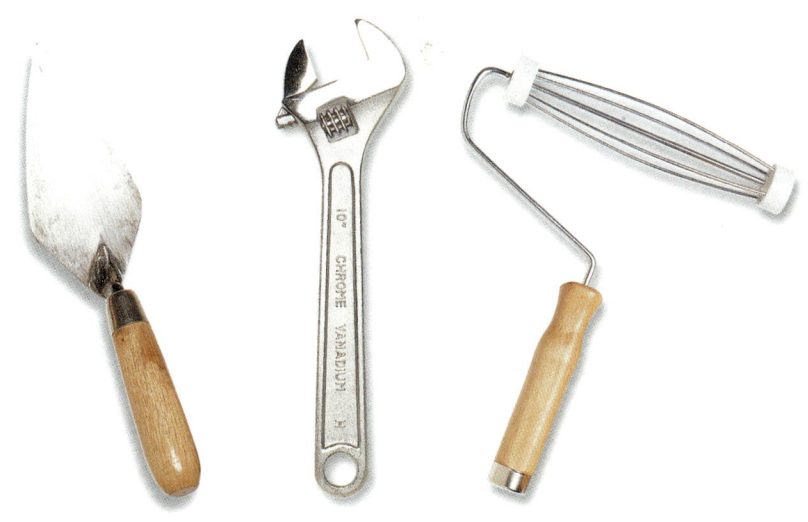

David Holloway

southwater

This edition is published by Southwater

Distributed in the UK by
The Manning Partnership
251–253 London Road East
Batheaston
Bath BA1 7RL
tel. 01225 852 727
fax 01225 852 852

Published in the USA by
Anness Publishing Inc.
27 West 20th Street
Suite 504
New York
NY 10011
fax 212 807 6813

Distributed in Canada by
General Publishing
895 Don Mills Road
400–402 Park Centre
Toronto, Ontario M3C 1W3
tel. 416 445 3333
fax 416 445 5991

Distributed in Australia by
Sandstone Publishing
Unit 1, 360 Norton Street
Leichhardt
New South Wales 2040
tel. 02 9560 7888
fax 02 9560 7488

Southwater is an imprint of
Anness Publishing Limited, Hermes House
88–89 Blackfriars Road, London SE1 8HA
tel. 020 7401 2077; fax 020 7633 9499

© Anness Publishing Limited 2002

10 9 8 7 6 5 4 3 2 1

Publisher: Joanna Lorenz
Managing Editor: Judith Simons
Art Manager: Clare Reynolds
Project Editor: Felicity Forster
Editor: Ian Penberthy
Photographer: Colin Bowling
Designer: Bill Mason
Editorial Reader: Penelope Goodare
Production Controller: Joanna King

Additional text: Brenda Legge

ACKNOWLEDGEMENTS AND NOTES
The publisher would like to thank *The Tool Shop*
for supplying the ladder for jacket photography:
97 Lower Marsh, Waterloo, London SE1 7AB
tel. 020 7207 2077; fax 020 7207 5222
www.thetoolshop-diy.com

The author and publishers have made every
effort to ensure that all instructions
contained within this book are accurate and
safe, and cannot accept liability for any
resulting injury, damage or loss to persons
or property, however it may arise. If in any
doubt as to the correct procedure to follow
for any home improvements task, seek
professional advice.

CONTENTS

INTRODUCTION

Even in the most temperate of climates, the weather can take an incredible toll on the structure of your home. The sun can crack and blister paintwork and the coverings of flat roofs; rain can soak into woodwork, causing it to rot, or seep into brickwork or behind flashings, penetrating the walls; a moist atmosphere causes fixings to rust and fail, leading to unsightly staining of walls, sagging gutters, missing roof tiles and broken

ABOVE: Carry out the majority of outdoor maintenance work during the summer months. The dry, warm conditions will make the tasks much less arduous.

fences; the wind can carry away or wreck all manner of structures; while the action of frost and snow can cause masonry and concrete to crumble. If you are to protect your home and its surroundings from the elements, you must be prepared to carry out regular outdoor maintenance and repairs.

The secret to keeping the outside of your home looking good is not letting things get out of hand. Don't delay

ABOVE: Guttering and downpipes are essential to carry away rainwater, preventing it from running down the walls and causing damage. They must be in good condition.

TIP

If you decide to make concrete yourself, consider buying a second-hand concrete mixer, and selling it again when the job is complete – it should save you money on buying or hiring costs.

when you see a problem; tackle it as soon as possible. Once a surface or finish outdoors begins to break down, the weather will quickly get in and speed up the process, turning a simple repair into a major project in no time. Fortunately, most outdoor maintenance and repair tasks require fairly basic skills, and they are not beyond the average do-it-yourselfer; structures tend to be of a rugged nature, requiring only a limited degree of finesse when it comes to finishing off.

Don't be over-confident, however. The weatherproofing and structural integrity of your home may depend on some tasks being done correctly, and some work may need to be carried out in fairly hazardous situations (on a roof for example). If you are in any doubt about completing a task successfully and safely, call in the experts.

ABOVE: The front door is often the first impression callers get of your home, so it pays to make sure that it is kept in good condition; that goes for the path, too.

RIGHT: Your home is a valuable investment, but it is under constant attack from the elements. You must carry out regular maintenance and repairs to prevent its fabric from deteriorating; once the weather gets in, it can cause untold damage. Fortunately, you don't need a lot of skill to carry out many outdoor tasks.

MATERIALS & EQUIPMENT

Outdoor repair and maintenance work can involve dealing with a variety of materials. Fortunately, most of the jobs you are likely to encounter are fairly straightforward and rarely require special tools. Any materials you choose must be rugged enough to withstand the weather. This is particularly true of fixings like nails and screws; there is a good range of sealants and adhesives formulated for outdoor use. Concrete and mortar are commonly found outdoors, too, so an understanding of these materials is essential. Safety is a major consideration outdoors, particularly as you may have to work from a ladder. If you intend using electric tools, you must take steps to prevent electrocution.

TOOLS

Much outdoor work will involve wood, so you must have a hammer for driving in nails, and a claw hammer is best because you can use it for extracting nails, too. Also include screwdrivers for screws with slotted and cruciform heads. Large sections of timber often have to be cut, so a good cross-cut saw is essential, while you can make cutouts with chisels. Choose a firmer chisel for heavy-duty work, mortise and bevel-edged chisels for getting into tight corners, and a plastic-handled chisel for driving with a mallet. A heavy-duty knife with a retractable blade will be invaluable for all manner of marking and trimming jobs.

You can use an electric drill outdoors with an extension lead (cord) protected by a circuit breaker, but a cordless drill will allow you to work anywhere.

Painting is a common outdoor task, so make sure you have a selection of brush sizes to cope with small and large areas. A roller will also be useful.

You may need to unscrew nuts and bolts, and if you don't have a selection of spanners (wrenches), arm yourself with a couple of adjustable spanners in different sizes. Pliers, too, are useful in this respect, and for a variety of other gripping jobs. If all else fails, you can cut through rusted bolts with a hacksaw.

For repairing mortar joints, you will need a small pointing trowel. A wallpaper seam roller is ideal for flattening flashing repair tape.

A spade and rake are essential for repairing asphalt (tarmacadam) drives.

heavy-duty pliers

slot screwdriver

heavy-duty retractable-blade knife

cordless drill

pointing trowel   **seam roller**

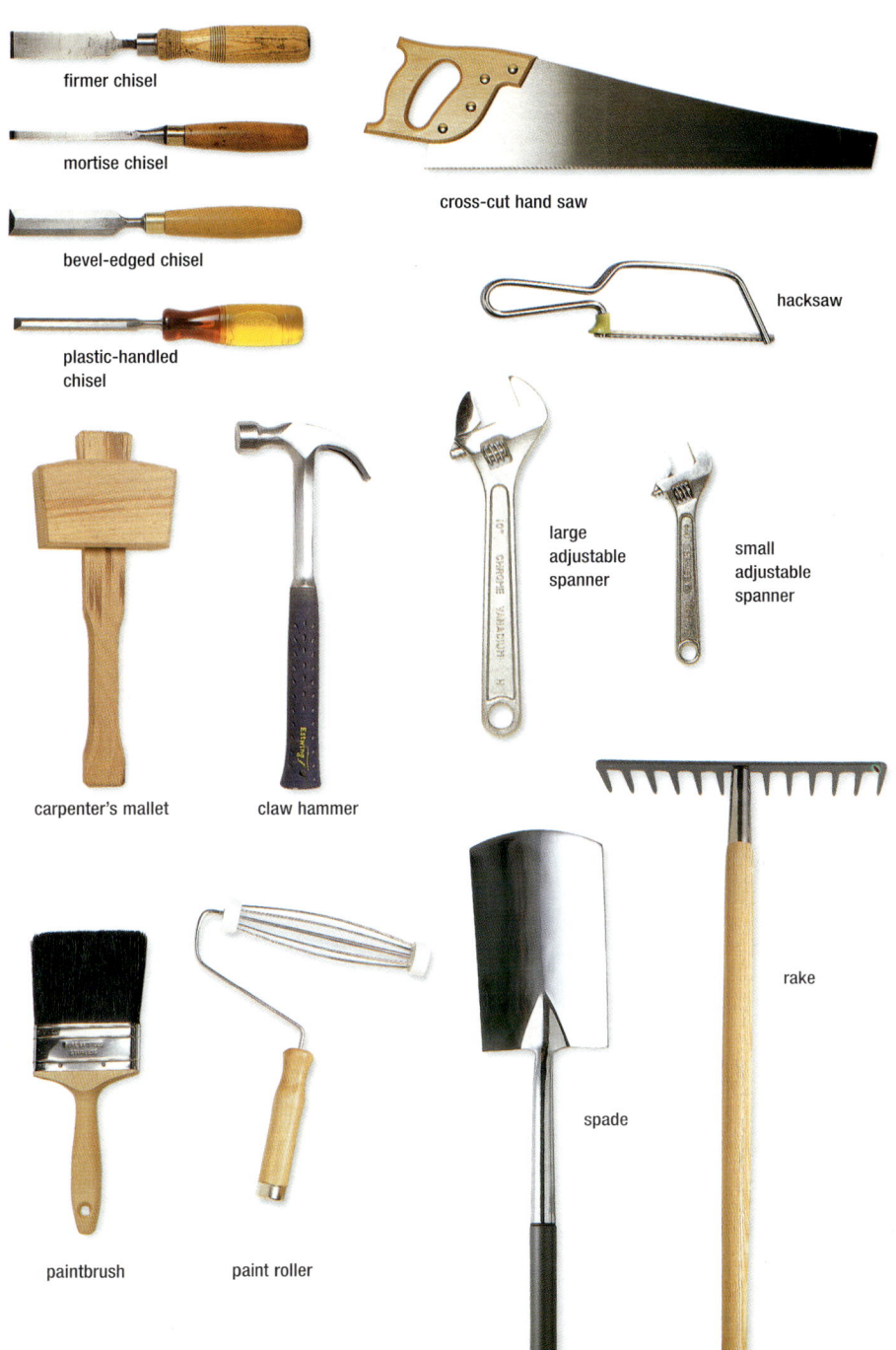

firmer chisel

mortise chisel

bevel-edged chisel

plastic-handled
chisel

cross-cut hand saw

hacksaw

large
adjustable
spanner

small
adjustable
spanner

carpenter's mallet

claw hammer

rake

spade

paintbrush

paint roller

NAILS, SCREWS AND DRILL BITS

There is no such thing as an "ordinary" nail. All nails have been designed for specific purposes, although some can be put to several uses.

Wire, lost-head and oval nails can be used for general carpentry. Oval nails can be driven below the surface of the work with less likelihood of them splitting the wood.

Cut nails have a tapering, rectangular section, which gives them excellent holding properties. They are largely used for fixing flooring.

Panel pins (brads) are used for fixing thin panels and cladding. They are nearly always punched below the surface, as are veneer pins.

When there is a need to secure thin or fragile sheet material, such as plasterboard (gypsum board), large-headed nails are used. These are commonly called clout nails, but may also be found under specific names, such as plasterboard nails.

The holding power of screws is much greater than that of nails, and items that have been screwed together can easily be taken apart again without damage to the components.

There are various types of screw head, the most common being the slotted screw head, followed by the Phillips head and the Pozidriv head, both of which have a cruciform pattern to take the screwdriver blade.

Drill bits come in a bewildering array of sizes and types but only a few are needed by the do-it-yourselfer, such as dowel bits for flat-bottomed holes, flat bits, which cut large holes very rapidly, and twist bits, which make small holes and are used for starting screws.

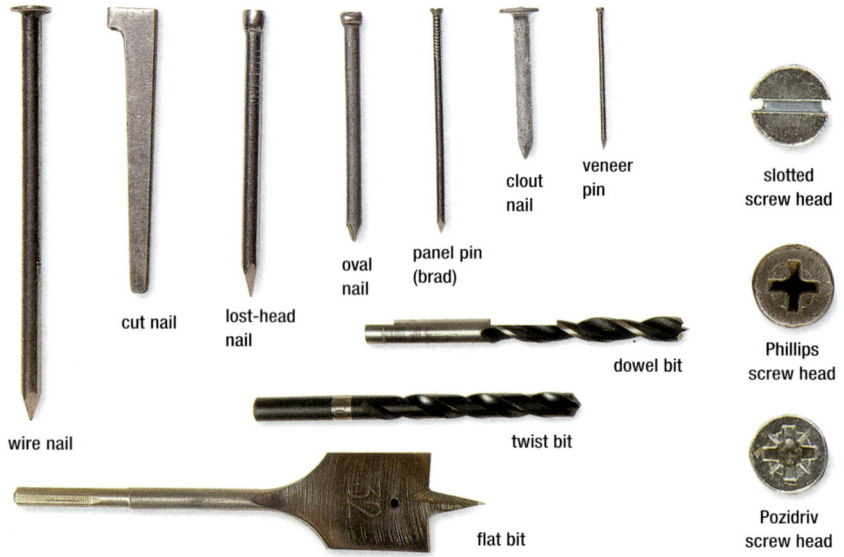

cut nail

lost-head nail

oval nail

panel pin (brad)

clout nail

veneer pin

wire nail

dowel bit

twist bit

flat bit

slotted screw head

Phillips screw head

Pozidriv screw head

ADHESIVES AND SEALANTS

A fantastic range of adhesives and sealants is available, some designed for specific uses, woodworking adhesive for example, and others formulated for general use. It is a good idea to keep a selection of both adhesives and sealants in your do-it-yourself armoury, so that you have them to hand in the event of an emergency repair situation.

WOODWORKING ADHESIVES

Most projects that require two or more pieces of wood to be glued together need a PVA (white) woodworking adhesive. This liquid dries quickly, loses its colour, and has the advantage that excess adhesive can be removed with a damp cloth before it sets.

Where a joint has to withstand damp conditions, an exterior-grade woodworking adhesive must be used. If the joint may need to be taken apart in the future, a traditional woodworking adhesive, such as animal glue or fish glue, can be used.

SEALANTS

The majority of sealants come in cartridges designed to fit into a caulking gun. This is an essential, but inexpensive, tool and is easy to use after a little practice. If you retain the tip that you cut off the end of the cartridge nozzle before you can use it, it can be reversed and used to seal the cartridge after use.

The most useful sealants for use outdoors are the building silicones and mastics (caulking), available in different colours and different grades depending on the final use. These have the advantage that they never set completely, so can be used for sealing between two materials that are likely to move slightly. A common example is the gap between a window or door frame and the surrounding brickwork.

Various repair sealants, often incorporating bitumen, are available for mending cracks in gutters, downpipes and flat roofs; expanding foam fillers can be used for sealing really large gaps.

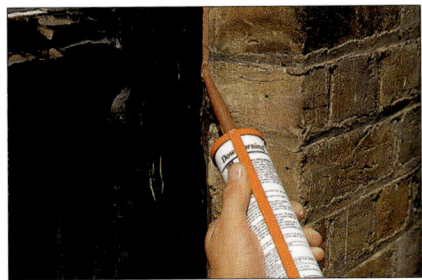

ABOVE: Use mastic (caulking) or silicone sealant outdoors to seal gaps between wood and masonry where a rigid filler might crack.

ABOVE: Use a non-setting mastic or coloured building silicone sealant to fill gaps around a door frame.

CONCRETE AND MORTAR

Concrete is used to provide a solid and rigid surface as a floor, as paving or as a base for a garage or outbuilding. Mortar is the "glue" that holds the bricks together in a wall. The basis for both concrete and mortar is cement and sand (fine aggregate); concrete also contains stones (coarse aggregate). When mixed with water, the cement sets to bind the aggregates solidly together.

CEMENT

Most cement used in the home is OPC (Ordinary Portland Cement). This is air-setting (that is, moisture in the air will cause it to harden unless bags are kept sealed and in the dry).

BUYING CONCRETE AND MORTAR

There are three ways of buying concrete and mortar: as individual ingredients, as wet ready-mixed and as dry pre-mixed. Buying cement, sand and coarse aggregate separately for concrete is the cheapest option, but you do have to ensure dry storage for the cement. For big jobs, having wet ready-mixed concrete delivered is convenient, provided sufficient manpower is available to transport it from the truck to the site and to level it before it sets. You also need to calculate the quantity needed accurately. For small jobs, bags of dry pre-mix are a good choice: the ingredients are in the correct proportions, and all you do is add water.

CONCRETE AND MORTAR MIXES

CONCRETE	mix	cement	sand	aggregate	yield*	area**
General-purpose	1:2:3	50kg	100kg	200kg	0.15	1.5
		(110lb)	(220lb)	(440lb)	(5.3)	(16)
Foundation	1:2½:3½	50kg	130kg	200kg	0.18	1.8
		(110lb)	(290lb)	(440lb)	(6.4)	(19.4)
Paving	1:1½:2½	50kg	75kg	150kg	0.12	1.2
		(110lb)	(165lb)	(330lb)	(4.2)	(13)

MORTAR	mix	cement	sand	lime***	yield*	bricks laid
Normal	1:5	50kg	200kg	50kg	0.25	850
		(110lb)	(440lb)	(110lb)	(8.8)	
Strong	1:4	50kg	150kg	15kg	0.19	650
		(110lb)	(330lb)	(33lb)	(6.7)	

* cubic metres (cubic feet) per 50kg (110lb) of cement
** area in square metres (square feet) of concrete 100mm (4in) thick
*** or plasticizer are optional - they can be added to the standard mix to improve workability

MIXING CONCRETE

1 Start by measuring out the dry ingredients in the right proportions.

2 Mix the dry ingredients thoroughly until you have a consistent colour.

3 Make a small well in the centre of the pile and add a small amount of water.

4 Work from the edges of the pile, mixing the ingredients and adding more water.

5 Work the material with the edge of your spade to get the right consistency.

6 When the concrete is mixed, transfer it to a bucket or wheelbarrow.

ACCESS EQUIPMENT AND SAFETY

Many do-it-yourself tasks have the potential to cause injury. Providing safe access to the work and following good working practices are essential.

LADDER SAFETY

Steps and ladders can be hazardous, so make sure they are in good condition. Accessories to make a ladder safer to use include the roof hook, which slips over the ridge for safety; the ladder stay, which spreads the weight of the ladder across a vertical surface, such as a wall, to prevent slippage; and the standing platform, which is used to provide a more comfortable and safer surface to stand on. The last often has a ribbed rubber surface and can be attached to the rungs of almost all ladders. Even more stable is the movable workstation or a board or

ABOVE: A ladder attachment that hooks over the ridge of a roof improves safety and avoids damage to the roof covering.

staging slung between two pairs of steps or trestles. These can often be used with a safety rail, which prevents the operator from falling even if a slip does occur.

ABOVE: A ladder platform will ensure a firm footing, especially if heavy footwear is worn.

ABOVE: Make sure that your ladder is secure at ground level. This is one of the most important steps to safe working practice.

LEFT: A simple circuit breaker can save a life. It works by cutting off the current as soon as an overload on the wiring is detected.

ELECTRICAL SAFETY

To safeguard against electrocution, which can occur if the flex (power cord) is faulty or is cut accidentally, the ideal precaution is a residual current device (RCD). This is simply plugged into the main supply socket (electrical outlet) before the flex and will give complete protection to the user. Extension leads can be purchased with automatic

TIPS

• Never over-reach when working on steps or a ladder; climb down and reposition it.
• Never allow children or pets into areas where power tools or strong solvents are being used.
• Do not work when you are over-tired. This causes lapses in concentration, which can lead to silly and/or dangerous mistakes.
• Keep the work environment tidy. Flexes (power cords) should not be walked on or coiled up tightly, because it damages them internally. Moreover, trailing flexes can be a trip hazard, and long extension leads can be prone to overheating.

USING PROFESSIONALS

As a do-it-yourself enthusiast, you have to be familiar with several trades, but it is often well worth employing a professional for structural work to save time and possibly money. There are many jobs, especially in plumbing and electrics, where professional help is welcome and indeed necessary. Professionals can also advise you in advance if your project is likely to fail for a reason you may not even have considered.

safety cutouts and insulated sockets, and these are ideal for both outside and inside work.

The danger of electrocution or damage caused by accidentally drilling into an existing cable or pipe can be largely prevented by using an electronic pipe and cable detector. This will locate and differentiate between metal pipes, wooden studs and live wires through plaster and concrete to a depth of approximately 50mm (2in). They are not too expensive and will be very useful for a variety of jobs inside and outside the home.

FIRST AID

It is inevitable that minor cuts and abrasions will occur at some point, so a basic first aid kit is another essential for the home or workshop. Keep your kit in a prominent position ready for use. If any of the contents are used, replace them immediately.

DRAINS, GUTTERS & ROOFS

Making sure that the drains, downpipes and guttering around your home are well maintained is essential to ensure that rainwater and waste water from indoors are carried away without having an opportunity to damage the structure. From time to time, however, pipes or gutters may become blocked, leading to an overflow. When that happens, you must be able to deal with the situation immediately, otherwise the results could be disastrous. Roofs are exposed to the full force of the weather and may, in time, become damaged: tiles may become dislodged, felt coverings may crack or blister, and flashings may deteriorate. Fortunately, all can be fixed with relative ease.

CLEARING DRAINS AND PIPES

A large auger can be used to clear blocked underground drains. It should be passed down through an open gully and along the drain until you reach the blockage.

The main soil pipe will run vertically either inside or outside the house. If it is blocked, your best chance of clearing it will be to unscrew an inspection hatch and then to use either an auger or drain rods to dislodge the blockage.

USING DRAIN RODS

These are used for clearing drains when there is a blockage between one (full) inspection chamber and the next (empty) one. When you discover the empty chamber, go back to the last full one and rod from there. Drain rod sets come with a choice of heads – plungers to push the blockage along the pipe, scrapers to pull it back and wormscrews or cleaning wheels to dislodge it.

Start with a wormscrew connected to two rods, lowering it to the bottom of the chamber. Feel for the half-round channel at the bottom of the chamber and push the wormscrew along this until it enters the drain at the end.

INSPECTING A SOIL PIPE

1 If you suspect that the blockage is in the vertical soil pipe, or at its base, begin by unscrewing an inspection hatch. Wear gloves and protective clothing.

Push it along the drain, adding more rods to the free end, and only turn the rods clockwise, otherwise they may become unscrewed. Keep working at the obstruction until water flows into the empty chamber, then use the scraper and plunger to clear the underground drain section.

wormscrew   cleaning wheel   scraper   plunger

2 Then remove the inner cover – make sure you are standing well out of the way, as the contents of the pipe will be discharged through the opening.

3 Use an auger or drain rods to clear the blockage before replacing the cover. Make sure it is tight, then flush the system through by turning on taps and flushing lavatory cisterns.

ABOVE: Use drain rods in an inspection chamber to remove a blockage. You can hire a set from a local tool-hire company; they will come with all the necessary fittings.

ABOVE: Use an auger in a waste gully at the foot of a drainpipe to clear a blockage. Alternatively, you may be able to shift it with the aid of a bent wire coat hanger.

CLEARING GUTTERS

The gutters and downpipes of your home are essential to remove rainwater. Nevertheless, they are exposed to the elements and are likely to become blocked, so regular maintenance is necessary to keep them clear and also to keep them in good condition.

Autumn is the ideal time to clear out gutters, removing leaves, birds' nests and general dirt and debris so that the winter rains can drain away freely. Use a garden trowel or gutter clearing tool to scoop out blockages from the gutters into a bucket, which should be secured to your ladder.

If there is a blockage near to the top of a downpipe, use something like a bent metal coat hanger to pull it out. Blockages farther down can be removed by using drain rods fitted with a wormscrew head.

LEFT: You can use a garden trowel to clean sediment and the remains of dead leaves from gutters. Protect downpipes temporarily with balls of screwed-up newspaper.

ABOVE: Alternatively, use a gutter cleaning tool specially designed for the job. You could even make your own from a length of broom handle with a piece of plywood screwed to the end. Cut the plywood so that it approximates the shape of the gutter profile and will clear the overhang of the roof covering.

REPAIRING GUTTERS

If a gutter is sagging, the most likely cause is failure of the screws that hold a bracket in place. First, remove the section of gutter above the offending bracket.

If the screws have worked loose, it may be possible to retighten them, perhaps replacing them with longer or larger screws; if the holes have become too large, move the bracket slightly to one side, making new holes in the fascia board for the bracket screws. Make sure it aligns with its neighbour. A rise-and-fall bracket is adjustable in height and so corrects sagging gutters without the need to remove them.

CAST-IRON GUTTERS

Traditional cast-iron gutters may look attractive, but they can give no end of trouble. To start with, they rust, so need regular painting to keep them looking good.

UNBLOCKING DOWNPIPES

You could fit a wire balloon into the top of a downpipe to prevent birds from nesting and to keep leaves and other debris out. If a downpipe gets blocked, clear it with drain rods fitted with a wormscrew.

PAINTING CAST-IRON GUTTERS

ABOVE: Prior to painting a cast-iron gutter, clear it out using a wire brush.

ABOVE: Treat cast-iron guttering with black bituminous paint to seal leaks.

REPAIRING CAST-IRON GUTTERS

ABOVE: If a cast-iron gutter bolt has rusted in place, you will not be able to unscrew it. Remove it by cutting through the bolt with a hacksaw.

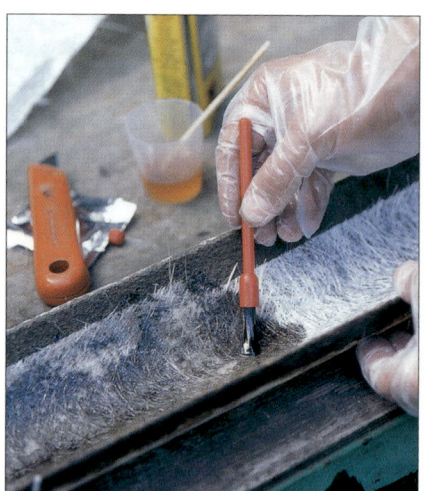

ABOVE: Wearing gloves, use glass fibre to repair a crack in a cast-iron gutter. Remove the gutter from the brackets to make it easier.

A more serious problem, however, is that the putty used to seal the joints can dry out, causing leaks.

You may be able to overcome minor joint leaks by cleaning the gutter out and brushing the inside with bituminous paint, but a proper repair will mean unscrewing the joint and replacing the old putty with non-setting mastic (caulking). Use a hacksaw to cut through the securing bolt if it has rusted in place. Then remove the screws holding the gutter to the fascia board and lift it clear. It will be very heavy – do not drop it, as it will shatter. Clean the joint faces, apply a layer of mastic and replace the gutter, using a new nut and bolt to connect the sections.

A crack or hole in a cast-iron gutter can be repaired with a glass fibre repair kit sold for use on car bodywork. Clean the damaged area thoroughly, then apply the glass fibre sheets over the damage and fill to the level of the surrounding metal with the resin filler provided with the kit. Glass fibre bandage can also be used in the same way for repairing cast-iron downpipes. Once it has cured, you can paint it as normal.

PLASTIC GUTTERS

Plastic guttering has largely replaced cast iron and is easier to repair. It is also much easier to replace because it is much lighter in weight and the joints simply clip together.

Leaks at the joints between lengths of plastic gutter are prevented by rubber seals, and if these fail it is usually quite easy to replace them. Take the old seal to the shop as a guide when buying a replacement. Otherwise, try cleaning them with some liquid soap to make them more efficient. If an end stop is leaking, replace the rubber seal in this in the same way.

The alternative is to use a gutter repair sealant, available in a cartridge for use with a caulking gun, forcing this into the joint to make a seal. Self-adhesive gutter repair tape is also available for sealing splits in plastic gutters and for covering small holes in gutters and downpipes.

When separating and reconnecting lengths of plastic guttering, note that some types simply snap into their securing brackets, while others have notches cut near the ends to take the clips. When fitting a new length, you will have to cut the notches with a hacksaw.

REPAIRING END STOPS

Rubber seals in the end stop of plastic guttering can be replaced if they fail.

REPAIRING PLASTIC GUTTERS

ABOVE: Gutter repair sealant can be used to fix a leaking joint between gutters.

ABOVE: Repair a crack in a gutter with gutter repair tape applied to the inside.

REPLACING ROOF SLATES

Slates that cover a pitched house roof can sometimes fail and work loose; you can repair small areas of damage yourself, but large-scale repairs may mean wholesale replacement of the roof covering, which should be entrusted to a professional roof contractor. Never walk directly on a roof covering; use a proper ladder that hooks over the ridge.

The most common cause of roof slates slipping is "nail sickness", that is one or both of the nails holding a slate has rusted through and snapped. The slate itself may be undamaged and still be on the roof somewhere.

If only one nail has failed, use a slate ripper to cut through the other one. This tool is slid under the slate, hooked around the nail and given a sharp tug to break the nail off or wrench it free of the batten (furring strip).

With the slate removed, you will be able to see, between the two exposed slates, one of the wooden battens to which the slates are attached. Cut a strip of zinc or lead sheet, about 150 x 25mm (6 x 1in), and nail one end of it to the exposed batten so that the strip runs down the roof.

Slide the slate back into its original position and secure it by bending the end of the zinc or lead strip over the bottom edge. Note that slates at the edges of the roof have mortar fillets beneath them to prevent the wind from blowing debris into the roof space. The mortar also prevents the edges from lifting in strong winds.

1 Use a slate ripper to cut through a slate nail that is still holding the slate.

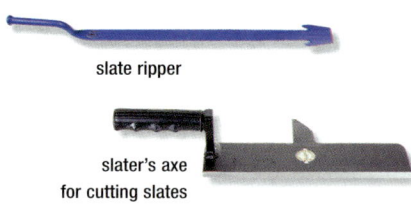

slate ripper

slater's axe
for cutting slates

REPLACING A DISLODGED TILE

Most concrete and many clay tiles are held in place by hooks, or nibs, on the top edge, which fit over the roof battens. If these are still intact, a dislodged tile can simply be replaced by gently lifting the surrounding tiles, supporting them on wooden wedges and slipping the tile back into position. If the nibs have broken off, the tile can be replaced in the same way as a slate. Edge tiles also have a fillet of mortar beneath them.

2 Slide out the damaged slate by lifting it with the blade of a trowel, taking care not to let it fall to the ground. Look for the batten (furring strip) between the exposed slates.

3 Fit a narrow strip of lead or zinc sheet in place by nailing one end of it to the batten under the slates. Use a galvanized nail and leave the strip running down the roof.

4 Slide the old (or replacement) slate into place over the lead or zinc strip. It may help to lift the slates in the course above by inserting wooden wedges beneath them.

5 Align the bottom edge of the slate with its neighbours, then bend the end of the strip over the bottom edge of the slate to hold it securely in place.

RIDGE TILES AND VALLEYS

On a pitched roof, ridge tiles and valleys seal the junctions between the faces of the roof.

RIDGE TILES

The curved tiles that run along the top of a tile or slate roof are mortared into place. With age and weathering, one or two may have become loose.

To replace ridge tiles, you need a roof ladder with hooks that fit over the ridge and wheels that allow you to run it up the roof from the top of a conventional ladder.

Once you have reached the ridge, remove the loose tiles, then use a small trowel to scrape away crumbling mortar until you reach sound mortar. Dampen the tiles and trowel on a bed of fresh mortar. Place each ridge tile gently into position, tapping it down with the handle of the trowel. Add mortar to the ends of each ridge tile to fill the joints with its neighbours.

VALLEYS

If you have a dual-pitch roof – different parts of the roof pointing in different directions – there will be a lead-lined valley between them to allow rainwater to escape and provide a junction between the tiles.

A severely damaged roof valley will need to be replaced completely – a job for professionals. But simple cracks can be repaired with self-adhesive flashing tape. Once the area around the crack has been cleaned, the tape is applied and rolled out flat using a seam roller.

REPLACING RIDGE TILES

1 If a ridge tile is loose, carefully lever it free and place it safely to one side. Clean away debris and apply a fresh bed of mortar.

REPAIRING VALLEYS

1 Clear out any leaves and debris from a leaking roof valley using a stiff brush. Wash off the lead and allow to dry completely.

2 Soak the old (or replacement) ridge tile in water, then place it in position, pushing it firmly down into the mortar.

3 With the ridge tile firmly in place and level with its neighbours, fill the joints with mortar and trowel them off to a neat finish.

2 Roll out self-adhesive flashing tape to repair the roof valley. In some cases, you may need to apply a special primer first.

ABOVE: Lead flashing is used to seal between a pitched roof and a parapet wall. It should be secured in a mortar joint.

REPAIRING FELTED FLAT ROOFS

Unless expensive materials have been used, the average life of a felted flat roof is about 10 to 15 years. If a felted flat roof fails, it is not worth trying to repair it and you should re-cover it. However, there are things you can do to repair minor faults and to extend the roof's life.

REPAIRING CRACKS AND BLISTERS

You will need bituminous mastic (caulking) to repair a crack or blister in a felted flat roof. Although quite messy, the job is straightforward.

First remove any loose chippings from around the damaged area with a brush. Using a hot-air gun, soften the felt first if necessary, and brush or scrape away dirt, moss and any other debris. With a crack or split in the roofing felt, pull back the edges; with a blister, make a cross-shaped pattern of cuts in the centre of the blister and peel back the four sections. If any seams are lifting, clean the area below them.

When the underlying surface has dried out, apply mastic to the exposed area and press down the edges of the crack, blister or lifted seam, using a wallpaper seam roller. If a crack cannot be closed up, use polyester reinforcing tape or flashing tape to strengthen the repair.

Some emergency roof repair compounds can be used to seal a leaking roof even if it is wet or under water. Instant repair aerosols can be used on damp roofs; check the manufacturer's instructions.

PATCHING A BLISTER

1 When tackling a damaged flat roof, brush all solar-reflective chippings, and dirt and debris away from the area to be repaired. This will show the extent of the damage.

SOLAR SEAL

A solar-reflective roof seal will absorb less heat and will remain more flexible, preventing the formation of blisters.

2 If necessary, use a hot-air gun to soften the damaged roofing felt before lifting the edges with a scraper. Clean the area beneath the damage and allow to dry out.

3 If the roofing felt has formed a blister, cut a cross shape in it with a sharp knife. Carefully fold back the triangular flaps of felt to expose the structure below.

4 When the damaged area is dry, apply the repair mastic (caulking) with a small brush, working it under the flaps of felt. Be generous to ensure a waterproof seal.

5 Self-adhesive flashing tape can be applied to cover up a crack that will not close up. Make sure it is pressed down firmly, particularly around the edges.

RE-PROOFING FELTED FLAT ROOFS

If a felted flat roof has several cracks or blisters, or is in bad condition generally, it is possible to waterproof it with either a bituminous emulsion or a longer-lasting elastomeric liquid rubber.

The whole roof should be swept clean before treating the surface with fungicide to kill any mould. Carry out any local repairs, then apply emulsion or liquid rubber.

Some bituminous emulsions require a priming coat before applying the main coat; all liquid rubber compounds are one-coat treatments.

When the emulsion or liquid rubber has dried, reapply stone chippings. Use new chippings if the old ones are dirty or have lost their shine – their purpose on a flat roof is to keep it cool by reflecting sunlight.

1 Sweep the whole roof clear and treat the surface with fungicide. Slit open blisters, allow the interior to dry and stick the flaps down with a layer of mastic (caulking).

2 Apply liquid rubber compound over the entire roof surface, spreading it evenly with a soft brush or broom.

3 Clean up splashes before they dry, and re-cover the roof with a good layer of loose stone chippings once the rubber compound has dried.

REPAIRING ROOF JUNCTIONS

The junction between a flat roof and the house wall is particularly prone to damage, allowing water to seep through. The correct way to seal this joint is with lead flashing, inserted into one of the mortar courses of the wall.

If a mortar fillet has been used to seal the junction, or if lead flashing has split, the simplest way to effect a repair is with self-adhesive flashing tape.

Clean the surfaces that are to be covered and apply any necessary primer before removing the backing paper and pressing down the flashing tape, first with your fingers, then a seam roller. Wear heavy gloves when doing this. The tape can be cut with scissors if required. Make good the mortar joints where any lead flashing meets the house wall, using fresh mortar.

1 You can use self-adhesive flashing tape to seal porous felt or metal flashings. In some cases, you may need to brush on a coat of special primer first.

2 Unroll the flashing tape, peel off the release paper and press the tape into position. Try to keep it as smooth and straight as possible.

3 Run a wallpaper seam roller firmly along both edges of the flashing tape to ensure that it bonds well.

PAINTING PIPES AND GUTTERS

New plastic pipes and gutters do not generally need to be painted. Older systems may be discoloured, however, in which case a coat of paint will rejuvenate them.

Clear away any rubbish that has built up and pour one or two buckets of water into the gutter to clean the system. Modern plastic gutters should require little additional preparation, but older cast-iron systems are prone to rusting, which can leave ugly deposits on brickwork and render. Remove the rust with a wire brush, clean the surface with turpentine, then lightly sand and remove all dust. Metal pipes and gutters should be primed, then a suitable undercoat and top coat applied. Begin at the top of the work area and work downward.

If the pipework and guttering have an existing bituminous paint finish, you will need to apply an aluminium primer before over-painting to prevent the old finish from bleeding through. When it comes to repainting the walls, any rust stains should be treated with a metal primer, otherwise they will show through the new finish. When the primer has dried, apply your decorative finish.

PAINTING PIPES

1 Start painting pipework from the top and work downward. This will prevent any dust or dirt you may disturb from dropping on to the newly painted surface and spoiling it.

2 Use card to protect the wall behind when painting downpipes. This will also prevent the brush from picking up bits of dust from the wall, which would mar the finish.

PAINTING BARGEBOARDS

A wealth of products has been developed for painting exterior woodwork. Never try to economize by using interior gloss paints outside; they will not cope with temperature extremes and will soon flake and split. Do not be afraid to experiment with bright colours on woodwork, but choose a finish that complements, rather than clashes with, other houses in the neighbourhood.

Choose a dry, calm day to paint and avoid working in direct sunlight, as the glare will prevent you from obtaining good, even coverage. Furthermore, if you are using a water-based (latex) paint, it will dry too rapidly, leaving hard edges.

Start by priming any bare areas, then apply an undercoat and finally one or two coats of gloss. With a standard gloss paint, begin by applying the paint vertically, and then use sideways strokes to blend it well. Work in the direction of the grain, blending in the wet edges for a uniform finish. If you are using a one-coat paint, apply the finish quite thickly in close, parallel strips and do not over-brush, as this will leave noticeable marks.

LEFT: Paint bargeboards early on in your work schedule. By starting from the top and working down you ensure that any dislodged dirt or paint droplets only fall on unpainted surfaces.

FENCES & WALLS

Making sure the fences and walls around your property are kept in good condition is essential. Not only do they provide a physical marker of the boundary, but also they prevent your children or pets from straying, ensure privacy and help keep out the uninvited. Most fences are made completely of wood, which can suffer considerably when exposed to the elements. A regular programme of maintenance and repair is essential if a wooden fence is to do its job properly. Even a masonry wall can deteriorate through the effects of weathering: bricks and mortar joints can crumble, while ground movement can lead to serious damage.

REPAIRING FENCE POSTS

A fence relies on its posts to provide much of its strength and to keep it upright – but because the posts are set in the ground and can get wet, they are prone to rotting, leading to the collapse of the fence.

The most vulnerable part of a fence post is the portion underground. Either this will be completely rotten, making the post unstable, or the post will have snapped off at ground level. In both cases, there are ways to effect a repair using the remaining sound piece of post.

If the fence post is still standing or is attached to a closeboard fence – overlapping vertical boards nailed to triangular-section horizontal (arris) rails – the best way to repair it is with a fence-post spur. This is a short concrete post that you set into the ground next to the broken post. Then you bolt the two together. Start by digging a hole roughly 30cm (1ft) square and 50cm (20in) deep in front of the broken post, that is on your side of the fence; you may need a long cold chisel and a club (spalling) hammer if you encounter concrete.

Place the spur in the hole so that it lines up with the post, then insert coach bolts in the holes in the spur, giving them a tap with a hammer to transfer their positions to the post. Drill holes in the post to take the bolts. Secure the spur to the fence post with the coach bolts and fill the hole around it, first with a layer of hardcore (rubble), ramming it down well so that there are no voids, then with a concrete collar. Trowel this off neatly. If necessary, prop the main post upright while the concrete sets.

With a panel fence, release the adjacent panels from the post and saw through it at ground level. Then hammer a repair spike – a shorter version of the normal fence-post spike – over the rotten wood in the ground. Fit the sound portion of the post into the socket of the spike and secure it with galvanized nails or rustproof screws. Finally, refit the fence panels to the posts.

POST LEVELS

A post level is a useful tool that can be strapped to a fence post to ensure that it is vertical in both directions when it is being installed.

FITTING A FENCE SPUR

1 With the fence still standing, dig a large hole – around 30cm (1ft) square – alongside the damaged post. Dig the hole to a depth of about 50cm (20in).

2 Place the concrete fence spur in the hole, setting it up against the post so that you can mark the positions of the coach-bolt holes ready for drilling.

3 Drill the holes in the damaged fence post, insert the coach bolts from the other side and secure the spur. Fit washers and nuts, and tighten the bolts with a spanner (wrench).

4 Fill the large hole first with hardcore (rubble) and then with concrete. Smooth down the surface and leave to set completely, supporting the post temporarily while it does so.

FITTING A REPAIR SPIKE

1 Remove the fence panels on each side of the damaged post. Then use a large saw, such as a bow saw or cross-cut saw, to cut off the post stump at ground level.

2 Position the repair spike carefully so that it is aligned with the remains of the old post. Using the spike driver and a sledgehammer, hammer in the repair spike over the rotten post.

POST SPIKES

Four different types of post spike. From the left: a normal post spike for new posts; a repair spike for rotten posts; a spike for mounting in fresh concrete; a spike for bolting down to a hard surface.

3 Insert the end of the new post into the spike socket, check that it is upright and secure it with galvanized nails or rustproof screws. Replace the fence panels.

REPLACING FENCE PANELS

A panel fence has posts regularly spaced at 1.83m (6ft) intervals. The panels come in a variety of designs – interwoven, overlapping and imitation closeboard are the most popular. They are all fixed between the posts in the same way: with either U-shaped metal clips or nails holding the panels to the posts.

If clips have been used, replacing a broken panel with a new one will be easy, since the panel is usually secured to the clips with screws. If the panel has been nailed in place, you may destroy it as you lever it out.

The new fence panel should fit exactly between the posts and can be secured in the same way. If the new panel is a tight fit at any point, use a planer-file or rasp to trim it; if it is loose, trim a section of the timber from the old panel to fill the gap.

1 To remove a fencing panel, start by levering out the nails holding it in place.

2 You may need to use a crowbar (wrecking bar) to lever out the panel.

3 If using clips to secure the new fence panel, nail these in place before sliding the panel through.

4 If using nails, drive them through the end section of the panel into the supporting post.

REPAIRING CLOSEBOARD FENCES

Timber fences are constantly exposed to the effects of rain, sun and wind. Sooner or later, parts of a fence will rot, split, break or simply fall off. Regular treatment with preservative or stain will prolong the life of a fence, but when repairs are necessary, do not delay, otherwise the fence will no longer do its job.

CLOSEBOARD FENCES

A closeboard fence consists of two or three horizontal triangular (arris) rails fitted between posts and supporting overlapping vertical lengths of tapered (feather-edge) boarding (pales). The result is an extremely durable and strong fence. Even so, arris rails can split and sag, while individual boards can become damaged.

A horizontal gravel board will run along the bottom of the fence to protect the end grain of the vertical boards from ground moisture. Normally, this is easy to replace, as it is held with just a couple of nails or screws.

Usually, a single broken board can be levered off with a claw hammer and the nails securing it prised out. If they will not budge, hammer them into the arris rail with a nail punch. Cut the replacement board to the same length and slide its thin edge under the thick edge of the adjacent board, having levered this clear of the arris rails slightly and removed the nails from it. Then nail through both boards – each nail holds two boards. If you are

replacing several boards, use a short piece of wood as a gauge to ensure even overlapping.

Make sure you treat the end grain at the foot of any new boards with preservative before they are nailed in place, as this will be very difficult to do once they are in position. You may want to treat the overlapping edges of the boards, too, as you won't be able to reach these either. Finish the job when the boards have been fitted.

Ideally, a closeboard fence should have capping strips nailed along the top to protect the end grain at the top of the boards from the weather. This is worth doing if your existing fence does not have them. Make sure the posts have caps that will shed water, too.

REPAIRING ARRIS RAILS

If an arris rail has split in the middle, you can buy a galvanized repair bracket that simply fits over the rail and is screwed or nailed in place. If necessary, have a helper lever the fence up, using a crowbar (wrecking bar) over a block of wood, while you fit the repair bracket.

A repair bracket that is similar, but with a flanged end, is available for reconnecting an arris rail that has broken where it is fixed to the fence post. This is screwed or nailed to both the rail and the post. You can use two of these brackets to replace a complete length of arris rail after sawing through the old rail at the ends and levering it from the fence.

REPAIRING CLOSEBOARD FENCING

1 Use an old chisel to lever out a damaged board in a closeboard fence. Prise out any nails that pull through the board, or drive them down into the arris rails.

2 Slide the replacement board into place, fitting its narrow edge beneath the adjacent board. Make sure the overlap is even, then nail the board to the horizontal arris rails.

3 You can reinforce a broken arris rail by nailing a galvanized steel repair bracket over the broken section. Use galvanized nails, as these will resist rusting.

4 Arris rails are tapered at their ends to fit slots cut in the posts, but this can weaken a rail. If an end breaks, nail a flanged galvanized repair bracket between the rail and the post.

REPAIRING GATES

If a wooden gate is sagging and dragging on the ground, check first that the posts are upright, using a level and paying particular attention to the hinged side. If a post has rotted, replace it with a new one.

If it is leaning slightly, it may be possible to force it back, with the gate removed, and ram some hardcore (rubble) or more concrete into the ground to hold it in place.

Wooden gates may also sag if the joints have become loose. You can fit a variety of metal brackets to support the framework of a wooden gate: flat L-shaped or T-shaped brackets at the corners where the vertical stiles meet the cross-rails or the diagonal brace, a right-angled bracket on the inside of the frame between stile and cross-rail,

and straight flat brackets to repair simple splits. All will look better if they are recessed into the wood. Alternatively, you could try replacing the main diagonal support brace or fitting longer hinges.

REPAIRING METAL GATES

First, check that the posts are vertical, then that you can move the adjusting nuts – often these will be rusted or clogged with paint. If this is the case, wire brush off the worst of the rust and paint, and apply a silicone spray or penetrating oil until you can turn the nuts freely. Finally, adjust the hinges so that the gate no longer rubs on the ground and swings freely, but closes properly.

REPAIRING A SAGGING GATE

ABOVE: Fit a replacement diagonal brace to support a wooden gate.

ABOVE: Using longer hinges is one way to secure a sagging wooden gate.

REPAIRING GARDEN WALLS

A common problem with garden walls is that bricks suffer from spalling, that is the surface breaks up. This results from water getting into the brick and expanding as it freezes.

Depending on how well the wall has been built, it may be possible to remove the damaged brick and turn it around, using a masonry drill and a thin-bladed plugging chisel to remove the mortar from the joints. However, it is likely that mortar on the back of the brick will prevent its removal. Therefore, the only solution will be to break it up with a bolster (stonecutter's) chisel and club (spalling) hammer, then insert a new brick. Remove all the old mortar from the hole, then lay a bed of fresh mortar on the bottom of the hole. Add mortar to the top and sides of the new brick and push it into place, forcing more mortar into the gaps. Finally, finish off the joints to the same profile as the remainder of the wall.

A garden wall can crack along mortar lines, and this often indicates a problem with the foundations. There is little alternative to demolishing at least the split section, investigating the problem and making good the foundations before rebuilding it.

REMOVING A DAMAGED BRICK

1 Remove the mortar around the old brick by drilling and chiselling it out.

2 Insert a new mortared brick, pushing it in until it is flush with its neighbours.

3 Repoint the mortar around the replaced brick to the correct profile.

REPOINTING BRICKWORK

Failed mortar joints between bricks are not only unsightly, but they also allow water into the wall, damaging the bricks when it freezes. The solution is to repoint the joints with fresh mortar.

First, use a thin-bladed plugging chisel to remove all the loose mortar until you reach sound material. Brush all the dust from the joints and dampen them with a paintbrush dipped in water or a hand-held garden sprayer.

Use a pointing trowel to push fresh mortar into the joints, working on the verticals first, then the horizontals. To do this, put a batch of mortar on a hawk – a flat metal plate or wooden board on a handle – then hold this against the wall directly beneath the joint you want to fill. Use the pointing trowel to slice off a thin strip of mortar and press it into the joint.

When you have used one batch of mortar, go back over all the joints, shaping the surface of the mortar to the required profile:

- Weatherstruck – using the edge of the pointing trowel to create a sloping profile that sheds rainwater from the wall. Start with the vertical joints and slope them all in the same direction.
- Recessed – using a square-shaped stick, or special tool.
- Flush – using sacking to rub the surface and expose the sand aggregate in the mortar.
- Concave (or rubbed) – using a rounded stick or a piece of hosepipe to make the profile.

A weatherstruck profile is often used on house walls for its rain-shedding properties, while recessed joints are only appropriate to wall surfaces inside. A concave profile is a good choice for garden walls.

ABOVE: The causes of cracked pointing should be investigated immediately and repaired. In some cases, it may be an indicator of serious problems with the foundations of the wall.

TIPS

- The secret of good repointing is to keep the mortar off the face of the brickwork. Take great care when forcing mortar into the joints, removing any excess immediately before it dries; clean off small splashes with a stiff brush.
- Let the joints harden a little before you give them a profile.
- Clean all bricklaying tools immediately after use with clean water. They will be much more difficult to clean if the mortar is allowed to dry.

1 Use a thin-bladed plugging chisel, or a small cold chisel, with a club (spalling) hammer to chop out all the loose mortar from the joints. Take care not to damage the edges of the bricks.

2 Brush any dust and debris from the joints and dampen the existing mortar with water. This will prevent the new mortar from drying too quickly, which would weaken it.

3 Load the hawk with a small amount of mortar and hold it tightly against the wall. Push narrow strips of mortar into the joints using a small pointing trowel.

4 Allow the mortar to "go off" slightly, then shape the pointing to the profile you want; in this case a concave profile is being obtained with a length of hosepipe.

PAINTING EXTERIOR WALLS

The best time to tackle exterior decorating is in early summer or autumn, when the weather is fine, but not too hot. Remember that this work will be on a much larger scale than an interior decorating project, so allow plenty of time to complete it. You may have to spread it over several weekends or perhaps take a week or two off work.

There is a wide range of paints available for painting exterior walls. Choose from cement paints, supplied as a dry powder for mixing with water, rough- and smooth-textured masonry paints, exterior-grade emulsion (latex) paints and exterior-grade oil-based paints for weatherboarding (siding). Masonry paints can typically be used straight from the can, but if you are painting a porous surface with a water-based product, it is advisable to dilute the first coat. Use a ratio of four parts paint to one part water.

Exterior paints come in a wide choice of colours, but exercise caution with some of the more flamboyant shades. White, cream, yellow, blue, green, soft pink and terracotta finishes, which are easy on the eye and blend into the background, are generally favoured by house buyers.

ABOVE: A typical example of pebbledash rendering. A coat of masonry paint can greatly improve its appearance. Use a brush with long bristles to get into all the cavities.

ABOVE: Avoid painting brickwork, if possible. Simply protect the face of the wall with a clear waterproofer. This will seal the surface and prevent water penetration.

PAINTING TECHNIQUES

ABOVE: Apply smooth masonry paint using a brush with coarse bristles.

ABOVE: You should apply textured masonry paint in the same way.

ABOVE: To protect downpipes from paint splashes, tape newspaper around them.

ABOVE: Use a banister brush to paint coarse exterior wall finishes such as pebbledash.

ABOVE: Choose a deep-pile roller for coarse surfaces and a medium one for others.

ABOVE: For speed, use a spray gun. Mask off surfaces you do not want painting.

PAINTING EXTERIOR WOODWORK

Exterior painted woodwork includes features such as fascias, soffits and bargeboards, as well as entire surfaces such as weatherboarding (siding). New woodwork should be sanded lightly, working with the grain. Remove any dust, then wipe with a cloth moistened with white spirit (paint thinner). Seal any knots with knotting solution (shellac), and fill holes or cracks. Existing paintwork should be washed down with a solution of sugar soap (all-purpose cleaner) and water, sanded and wiped off with a cloth moistened in white spirit. Scrape off flaking paint; any bare areas should be primed and undercoated in the normal way.

WINDOWS AND DOORS

Exterior windows and doors can be treated in much the same manner as other outdoor wood. Start by filling and

PAINTING A DOOR

1 Remove flaking paintwork, then smooth the surface with a palm sander.

2 Apply a suitable primer and allow to dry completely before over-painting.

3 Apply one or two undercoats and lightly rub down with abrasive paper between coats.

4 Apply topcoat to mouldings and panelled areas first, then move on to cross rails.

sanding any cracks or holes in the wood. Bare wood should be primed and undercoated, while old or defective paintwork will need sanding before over-painting. If the existing paintwork is badly cracked or blistered, it should be stripped off completely and a new primer, undercoat and top coat applied.

FENCES

For fences and outbuildings, there is a wide selection of exterior wood stains and paints in all shades. Many are water-based and plant-friendly, while being tough enough to withstand the rigours of quite harsh climates. Special paints and stains have also been developed for decking with a greater resistance to scuffing and cracking.

The best time to paint fencing is on a dry day in the late autumn, when many plants will have died back, making access easier. Brush off dirt and dust, and scrape soil away from the foot.

PAINTING A FENCE

ABOVE: Fences and gates can be painted in all shades of bright colours.

WEATHERBOARDS

For weatherboard (siding) surfaces, wash down with a solution of sugar soap. Leave to dry for a week. Replace any severely damaged sections and fill smaller cracks with a sealant (caulking). Punch in any protruding nails and cover with metal primer. Then prepare as for other woodwork.

PAINTING WEATHERBOARDS

1 It is easy to miss sections of weatherboarding (siding), so paint the undersides first.

2 Paint the facing boards next, and finish off with the end grain.

PATHS, DRIVES & PATIOS

The hard surfaces around your home –
paths, a drive and perhaps a patio – may be
paved in a variety of materials, but the most
common are concrete, slabs of stone or
concrete, concrete blocks and asphalt
(tarmacadam). Again, the weather and the
simple wear and tear of being walked on can
cause damage. This must be repaired
immediately, not only because it is likely to
spread, particularly if water gets in and
freezes during the winter, but also because a
damaged surface is a danger to walk on.
Making repairs to concrete is quite easy,
while any form of slab or block paving can
be fixed simply by lifting and replacing the
damaged sections. An asphalt surface can
be made good with a cold-cure repair pack.

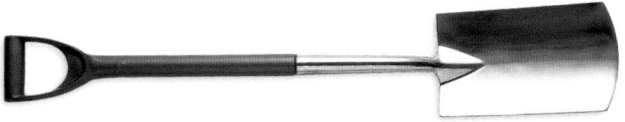

REPAIRING CONCRETE PATHS

There are many materials that can be used for surfacing paths, patios and drives, and in time most will need some form of repair or maintenance.

Concrete is a popular choice for paving because it is relatively cheap and easy to lay. Nevertheless, it can crack, develop holes and crumble at exposed edges.

Before carrying out any repairs to concrete paving, it is a good idea to clean it thoroughly, and the best way of doing this is to use a pressure washer, which directs a high-velocity jet of water at the surface, removing all algae, slime, dirt and debris. Chip out any damaged areas until you have a solid surface to work on.

Minor holes and cracks can be repaired with exterior filler, quick-setting cement or mortar made with fine sharp sand rather than soft builder's sand. However, you should chip out holes to a depth of about 20mm (¾in) and enlarge cracks to allow the repair compound to grip properly. Any repairs involving edges will require the use of timber shuttering to contain the repair compound while it dries. Fitting shuttering is fairly simple, using stout timber boards. Solid timber pegs are driven into the ground so that the boards fit tightly against the edge of the existing concrete.

Spread the repair compound over the damaged area – some PVA adhesive (white glue) brushed over the surface will help it stick – and smooth it out with a trowel.

1 Sweep the path clear of dead leaves and debris. Then clean the damaged area with a pressure washer to remove all ingrained dirt and algal growth.

Before the repair compound sets completely, lightly roughen the surface with a stiff brush, as smooth concrete surfaces are dangerous to walk on when wet.

Finally, remove the shuttering and smooth off any rough areas with the trowel and a piece of sacking.

TIP

Apart from brushing, there are several ways you can make a concrete surface more attractive and less slippery. Embedding small stones in the surface is one method, or you could provide surface texture with a plasterer's trowel or by rolling a heavy pipe over the concrete.

2 Fit a length of wood along the edge of the path and drive pegs into the ground to hold it in position. This will act as shuttering to retain the repair compound while it sets.

3 Mix up the concrete repair compound in a bucket with a small amount of water. Adding a little PVA (white) glue will improve adhesion. Soak the damaged area with water.

4 Use a plasterer's trowel to press the concrete into the damaged area. Smooth it off level with the top of the shuttering and the surrounding path. Roughen the surface lightly.

5 Allow the repair one or two days to dry, then remove the shuttering and pegs. It should come away easily, but if not, tap the wood gently with a hammer to jar it loose.

REPAIRING CONCRETE STEPS

Solid concrete steps are very prone to damage, especially at the edges. You need only a minimum of tools to carry out the necessary work, but make sure you have the right safety wear (gloves and safety shoes) and do not work in very cold weather.

Minor damage in a concrete step, such as small cracks and holes, can be repaired in much the same way as repairing cracks and holes in plaster walls, except that you use an exterior-grade filler, quick-setting cement or mortar made from three parts fine sharp sand to one part cement.

Brushing the damaged area with PVA adhesive (white glue) will help the repair compound to stick. Smooth off the surface of the repair compound with a trowel before it has finally set, as you will not be able to rub it down afterwards. Any repair involving a broken corner or edge, however, will require shuttering to contain the repair compound while it sets.

For small repairs to the edge of a step, you need only a block of wood propped in place; more extensive repairs need complete shuttering. Exterior-grade plywood is the best material for this. Use three pieces to make a three-sided mould of the correct height. Secure them at the back with timber anchor blocks screwed to wall plugs inserted in the wall alongside the step. For

1 Use a wire brush to remove loose and damaged concrete around the step. You may need to clean up the damaged area with a cold chisel and club (spalling) hammer.

freestanding garden steps, secure the shuttering in place with sash clamps.

Before fitting the shuttering, use a wire brush to remove any loose concrete and plant matter from the step. Hack off any split pieces of concrete and then brush the surface with PVA adhesive.

With the shuttering in place, trowel in the repair compound and smooth it off, using the top of the shuttering as a guide. As it begins to dry, when moisture has disappeared from the surface, roughen the surface with a stiff broom or hand brush. Then use a small pointing trowel to round off the edges where they meet the shuttering. Remove the shuttering when the filler, cement or mortar has set.

2 Apply a coat of PVA adhesive (white glue) to the surface to help the repair compound stick. Add a little to the water when mixing the repair concrete.

3 Fit a length of wooden shuttering to the step edge to retain the new concrete while it sets. This can be held in place by means of wooden props or pegs, or even screwed to the step.

4 Using a small trowel, fill the damaged area in the step edge with repair concrete and smooth it out. Make sure it is level with the top of the wooden shuttering.

5 Once the concrete has dried a little, give it a non-slip finish to match the surrounding surface and trowel off the sharp corner. Allow to dry completely, then remove the shuttering.

REPAIRING ASPHALT PATHS

Asphalt (tarmacadam) is an economical and hardwearing paving material. Provided it has been laid properly, an asphalt path or drive can last a long time.

However, many domestic asphalt paths and drives may have been laid badly and may start to crumble. If weeds begin to break through the surface, it is a sign that an insufficient thickness of asphalt has been laid, and the only sensible answer is to have a second layer professionally installed on top of the existing one. Laying a complete asphalt drive, which needs to be done with hot asphalt, is not a job for the amateur. However, small holes can be readily mended without professional assistance.

The first step is to sweep the existing drive thoroughly, paying particular attention to the area around the intended repair. If the surface adjacent to the damage has become distorted, you may be able to reshape it by heating the surface with a hot-air gun and tamping the asphalt down with a piece of wood.

Cold-lay asphalt repair compounds are normally laid after the application of a coat of bitumen emulsion.

Compact the repair compound into the hole or depression, using a stout piece of wood or a garden roller for a large area. Spray the roller with water to prevent the repair compound from sticking to it. If you want, scatter stone chippings over the asphalt and roll them in.

1 Sweep the damaged area of the path or drive to remove all dirt, dead leaves and loose particles of asphalt (tarmacadam). You must have a clean working area.

Really deep holes should be filled partially with concrete before adding the final layer of cold-fill compound.

GOOD DRAINAGE

If there are puddles forming on your paving or if rainwater does not clear away, it is a sign that the paving has not been laid to the correct slope (fall).

This does not need to be huge, and around 1 in 100 is recommended, that is 1cm per metre (½in per 3ft). The fall can be checked using a straight wooden batten set on edge with a small block of wood under its lower end and a spirit (carpenter's) level on top. The thickness of the wood block depends on the length of the batten; for a 3m (10ft) batten, you need a 30mm (1¼in) block.

2 Apply asphalt repair compound and press it into the damaged area with a spade or trowel. You may need to treat the area of the repair with a bitumen emulsion first.

3 Tamp down the filled area with a stout piece of wood or use a garden roller to flatten it. If necessary, add extra asphalt to bring the level of the repair up to the surrounding surface.

4 Large areas of asphalt often have contrasting stone chippings bedded in the surface to break up the expanse of single colour. These can be sprinkled on the repair and rolled in.

SAFETY FIRST

• Many paving materials, especially paving slabs, are heavy and have rough edges. So it is important that you wear the correct safety gear to avoid injuries to your hands and feet – stout gloves and safety shoes are a minimum. Gloves will also provide some protection for your hands when using heavy hammers.

• If you are not strong enough, do not attempt to lift paving slabs by yourself as you could damage your back. When lifting, always bend your knees and keep your back straight.

• Take care, too, when using tools such as angle grinders for cutting paving slabs to fit in corners and other awkward areas.

REPAIRING CONCRETE SLAB PAVING

Concrete paving slabs are a common choice of surfacing for patios. The same slabs can also be used for paths, but for drives, stronger and thicker, hydraulically pressed slabs must be laid on a much stronger base. Normally, paving slabs are set on dabs of mortar on a sand base, but they may also be laid on a solid bed of mortar, a method that is always used when laying heavy-duty slabs for a drive.

A slab may have broken because something too heavy has been placed on it or as a result of something hitting it. Sometimes, individual slabs may become loose or may sink, in which case they will need to be lifted and re-laid.

If the joints around the slab have been filled with mortar, the first job will be to chip this out.

If possible, remove a broken slab from the centre, working outward; you can use a bolster (stonecutter's) chisel or a garden spade to lever up sections or whole slabs. Clean out the bottom of the hole and level it using builder's sand tamped down with a stout piece of wood – allow about 10mm (³⁄₈in) for the mortar. Mix up a batch of mortar and put down five dabs, one in the centre and one near each corner. Also lay a fillet of mortar along each edge.

Lower the new slab, or the old slab if it is undamaged, into position and tap it down with the handle of a club (spalling) hammer. Check that the slab is level with its neighbours by placing a spirit (carpenter's) level across them. Fill the joints with more mortar.

1 Use a narrow-bladed masonry chisel and club (spalling) hammer to chip out the mortar around a damaged paving slab. Be careful not to chip the edges of neighbouring slabs.

4 Lower the replacement paving slab into position, making sure that it lines up with the surrounding slabs and that there is an even gap all around.

2 Lift out the broken pieces, or lever them up with a bolster (stonecutter's) chisel or spade, but protect the edges of adjoining slabs with pieces of wood.

3 Clean out the hole, removing all the old mortar. Add more sand, tamping it down well, then trowel in five blobs of mortar and apply a thin strip of mortar around the edges.

5 Use the handle of your club hammer to tap the slab down until it is exactly level. Check by laying a long spirit (carpenter's) level or a straightedge across the slabs.

6 Add some more mortar to finish the joints, smoothing it down level with the paving. Brush off the excess immediately, otherwise it will stain the surface of the paving.

REPAIRING CONCRETE BLOCK PAVING

Concrete blocks are commonly used for paving: the individual blocks are bedded in a layer of sand and held tightly against one another by edging blocks or restraints set in mortar. Fine sand is brushed into the joints between the blocks.

Because the blocks will be packed so tightly together, a damaged block will have to be broken up to remove it.

1 Use the largest masonry bit you possess to make a hole with a hammer drill in a damaged paving block. Several holes would be even better.

2 Use the hole as a starting point for chipping out the block with a cold chisel and club (spalling) hammer. Wear eye protection.

3 Clean up the hole, then add a little more sand to the bottom. Level it off with the edge of a short length of wood.

4 Push the new block into place. Tamp it down until it is level with the surrounding blocks, using a length of wood to protect it.

REPAIRING CRAZY PAVING

This form of paving employs pieces of real stone or broken slabs (whole slabs of real stone are prohibitively expensive) and is popular for paths, although larger areas may also be paved in this manner. It can be laid in one of two ways: on a bed of sand or a bed of concrete. Like full-size paving slabs, individual pieces may break, sink or work loose.

When repairing crazy paving, you may need to re-lay quite large areas. As when laying new crazy paving, work from the sides toward the centre, using the biggest pieces with the straightest edges along the sides, then filling in with smaller pieces.

Whichever way you lay crazy paving, the joints should always be well mortared, and the mortar finished flush or shaped with a pointing trowel to give V-shaped grooves around the slab.

If an individual block becomes damaged, the main problem will be getting it out to replace it. Drill holes in it with the largest masonry drill you own, then break it up with a cold chisel and club (spalling) hammer. In this way, you will reduce the risk of damaging the surrounding blocks. Loosen the sand at the base of the hole and add a little more so that the new block sits proud of the surface by around 10mm ($\frac{3}{8}$in). Tap it down with the handle of the club hammer, then force it into its final position by hitting a stout piece of wood laid over the block with the head of the hammer. Brush fine sand into the joints.

ABOVE: Crazy paving paths can be both functional and attractive. You may need to re-lay large areas when laying new slabs.

CLEANING PAVING

A pressure washer is the most effective way of cleaning paving, but you need to be careful not to splash yourself (wear protective clothing in any case) and not to wash earth out of flowerbeds. Never point the spray directly at the house walls.

INDEX

The publisher would like to thank
the following for supplying
pictures: Axminster 26 (cutouts);
DIY Photo Library 34bl, 59bl; HSS
Hire Tools 16br; Hunter Plastics
6b, 7b, 16t.